	DATE DUE		

South America

by
Fran Sammis

BENCHMARK **B**OOKS

MARSHALL CAVENDISH
NEW YORK

Marshall Cavendish Corporation
99 White Plains Road
Tarrytown, New York 10591-9001

© Marshall Cavendish Corporation 2000

Series created by Blackbirch Graphics, Inc.

Photo Credits

Page 13: ©Brent Winebrenner/International Stock; page 18: ©André Hote/
International Stock; pages 19 and 37 (gold mask): ©Buddy Mays/International
Stock; pages 37 (Machu Picchu) and 56: Roberto Arakaki; page 40: North Wind
Picture Archives; pages 54 and 58: © Chad Ehlers/International Stock

Printed in Hong Kong

Library of Congress Cataloging-in-Publication Data

Sammis, Fran.
    South America / by Fran Sammis.
        p.   cm. — (Mapping Our World)
    Includes bibliographical references and index.
    Summary: Text, photographs, and maps introduce information about the cli-
mate, land use, resources, plants and animals, population, politics, and religions of
South America.
    ISBN 0-7614-0369-8
    1. Cartography—South America—Juvenile literature. [1. Cartography—South
America 2. South America—Maps.] I. Title. II. Series: Sammis, Fran. Mapping
our world.
    GA641.S26   1999
    980—dc21   98-28887
                                                                              CIP
                                                                              AC

Contents

160°

180°

160°

140°

120°

100°

80°

60°

40°

100°

80°

60°

20°

40°

60°

0°

20°

40°

20°

0°

80°

60°

40°

20°

Tropic of Cancer

20°

0°

EQUATOR

20°

Tropic of Capricorn

40°

60°

4

The Importance of Maps

As tools for understanding and navigating the world around us, maps are an essential resource. Maps provide us with a representation of a place, drawn or printed on a flat surface. The place that is shown may be as vast as the solar system or as small as a neighborhood park. What we learn about the place depends on the kind of map we are using.

Kinds of Maps

Physical maps show what the land itself looks like. These maps can be used to locate and identify natural geographic features such as mountains, bodies of water, deserts, and forests.

Distribution maps show where something can be found. There are two kinds of distribution maps. One shows the range or area a feature covers, such as a map showing where grizzly bears live or where hardwood forests grow.

The second kind of distribution map shows the density of a feature. That is, how much or how little of the feature is present. These maps allow us to see patterns in the way a feature is distributed. Rainfall and population maps are two examples of this kind of distribution map.

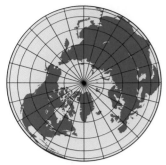
Globular

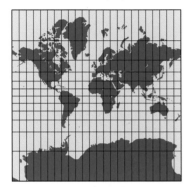
Mercator

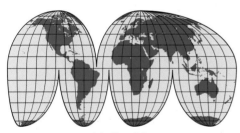
Mollweide

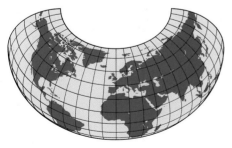
Armadillo

Political maps show us how an area is divided into countries, states, provinces, or other units. They also show where cities and towns are located. Major highways and transportation routes are also included on some kinds of political maps.

Movement maps help us find our way around. They can be road maps, street maps, and public transportation maps. Special movement maps called "charts" are used by airplane or boat pilots to navigate through air or on water.

Why Maps Are Important

Many people depend on maps to do their jobs. A geologist, for example, uses maps of Earth's structure to locate natural resources such as coal or petroleum. A transportation planner will use population maps to determine where new roads may need to be built.

A map can tell us how big a place is, where one place is in relation to another, what a place was like in the past, and what it's like now. Maps help us understand and move through our own part of the world and the rest of the world, too. Some maps even help us move through our solar system and universe!

Terms to Know

Maps are created and designed by incorporating many different elements and accepted cartographic (mapmaking) techniques. Often, maps showing the exact same area will differ from one another, depending upon the choice or critical elements, such as scale and projection. Following is a brief listing of some key mapmaking terms.

Projection. A projection is a way to represent the round Earth on a flat surface. There are a number of different ways to project, or transfer, round-Earth information to a flat surface, though each method results in some distortion. That is, areas may appear larger or smaller than they really are—or closer or farther apart. The maps on page 6 show a few varieties of projections.

Latitude. Lines of latitude, or parallels, run parallel to the equator (the imaginary center of Earth's circumference) and are used to locate points north and south of the equator. The equator is 0 degrees latitude, the north pole is 90 degrees north latitude, and the south pole is 90 degrees south latitude.

Longitude. Lines of longitude, or meridians, run at right angles to the equator and meet at the north and south poles. Lines of longitude are used to locate points east and west of the prime meridian.

Prime meridian. An imaginary line that runs through Greenwich, England; considered 0 degrees longitude. Lines to the west of the prime meridian go halfway around the world to 180 degrees west longitude; lines to the east go to 180 degrees east longitude.

Hemisphere. A half circle. Dividing the world in half from pole to pole along the prime meridian gives you the eastern and western hemispheres. Dividing the world in half at the equator gives you the northern and southern hemispheres.

Scale. The relationship of distance on a map to the actual distance on the ground. Scale can be expressed in three ways:

    1. As a ratio—1:63,360 (one inch equals 63,360 inches)

    2. Verbally—one inch equals one mile

    3. Graphically— [1 mi.   ]

Because 63,360 inches equal one mile, these scales give the same information: one map-inch equals one mile on the ground.

Large-scale maps show a small area, such as a city park, in great detail. Small-scale maps show a large area, such as an entire continent, in much less detail, and on a much smaller scale.

The Art and Process of Mapmaking

Maps have been made for thousands of years. Early maps, based on first-hand exploration, were some of the most accurate tools of their

◄◄ *Opposite: The maps shown here are just four of the many different projections in which the world can be displayed.*

225 million years ago

1

180 million years ago

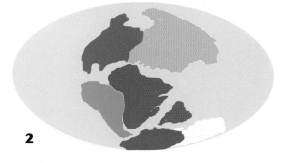

2

65 million years ago

3

present day

4

time. Others, based on guesses about what an area was like, were often very beautiful, but were not especially accurate.

As technology—such as photography and flight—evolved, cartographers (mapmakers) were able not only to map most of Earth in detail, they were also able to make maps of our solar system.

To make a map today, cartographers first determine what a map is to show and who is most likely to use it. Then, they assemble the information they will need for the map, which can come from many different kinds of experts—such as meteorologists, geologists, and surveyors—as well as from aerial photography or satellite feedback.

Mapping a Changing Earth

If you traced around all the land masses shown on a world map, then cut them out and put them together like a jigsaw puzzle, the result would look something like map 1 at the top of this page. Scientists think this is how Earth looked about 225 million years ago.

Over time, this single continent, Pangaea (Pan–JEE–uh), slowly broke apart into two land masses called Laurasia and Gondwanaland (map 2). Maps 3 and 4 show how the land masses continued to break up and drift apart over millions of years, until the continents assumed the shapes and positions we recognize today. Earth has not, however, finished changing.

Scientists have established that Earth's surface is made up of sections called tectonic plates. These rigid plates, shown in the map on page 9, are in

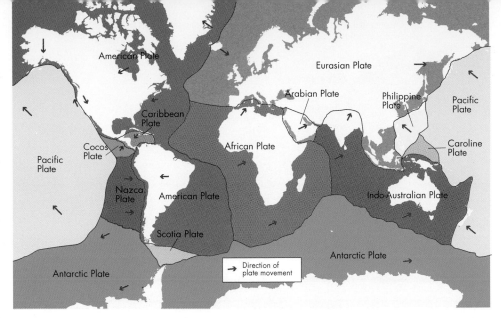

◀ *Left:* The tectonic plates that lie beneath Earth's surface are in a slow but constant motion.

◀◀ *Opposite:* The continents of our planet were once clumped together but have spread apart over millions of years in what is called continental drift.

slow, constant motion, moving from 1/4 to 1 inch a year. As they move, they take the continents and sea floors with them. Sometimes, their movements cause disasters, such as earthquakes and volcanic activity.

After many more millions of years have passed, our Earth's continents will again look very different from what we know today.

Reading a Map

In order for a map to be useful, it must be the right kind of map for the job. A small-scale map of Illinois would not help you find your way around Chicago; for that, you would need a large-scale map of the city. A physical map of North America would not tell you where most of the people live; you would need a distribution map that shows population.

Once you have found the right map, you will need to refer to the map legend, or key, to be sure you are interpreting the map's information correctly. Depending on the type of map, the legend tells the scale used for the map, and notes the meaning of any symbols and colors used.

In their most basic form, maps function as place finders. They show us where places are, and we use these maps to keep from getting lost. But as you have begun to see, maps can tell us much more about our world than simply where places are located. Just how much more, you'll discover in the chapters ahead.

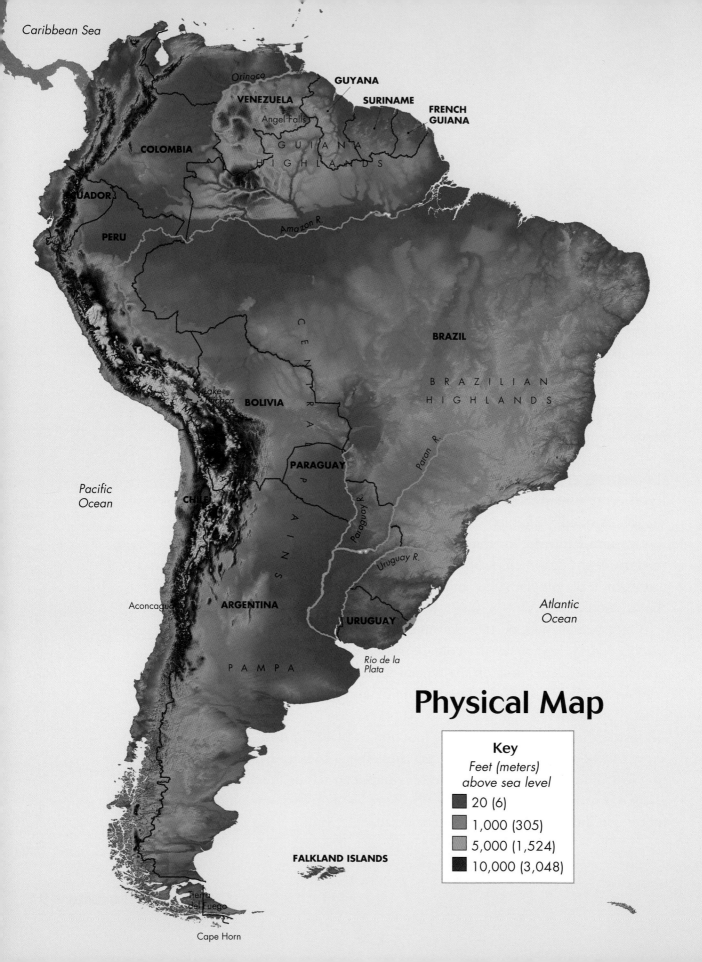

Caribbean Sea

Orinoco

GUYANA

VENEZUELA

SURINAME

Angel Falls

**FRENCH
GUIANA**

COLOMBIA

G U I A N A
HIGHLANDS

EUADOR

Amazon R.

PERU

BRAZIL

B R A Z I L I A N
H I G H L A N D S

C
E
N
T
R
A
L

Lake
Titicaca

BOLIVIA

A

Paran R.

PARAGUAY

P
L
A

Paraguay R.

I

Pacific
Ocean

CHILE

N
S

Uruguay R.

Atlantic
Ocean

Aconcagua

ARGENTINA

URUGUAY

Rio de la
Plata

Physical Map

P A M P A

FALKLAND ISLANDS

Key
Feet (meters)
above sea level

⬛	20 (6)
⬛	1,000 (305)
⬜	5,000 (1,524)
⬛	10,000 (3,048)

Tierra
del Fuego

Cape Horn

1
Mapping Natural Zones and Regions

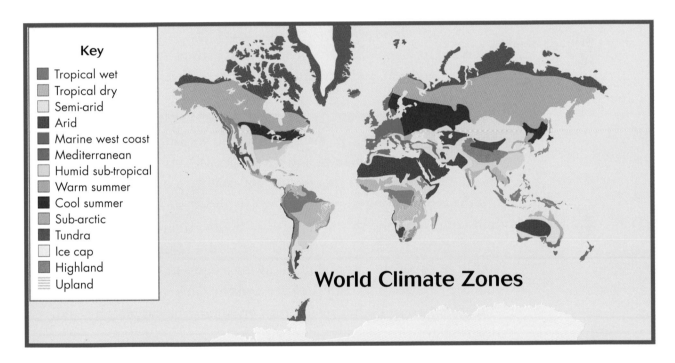

Key

- ■ Tropical wet
- ■ Tropical dry
- □ Semi-arid
- ■ Arid
- ■ Marine west coast
- ■ Mediterranean
- □ Humid sub-tropical
- ■ Warm summer
- ■ Cool summer
- ■ Sub-arctic
- ■ Tundra
- □ Ice cap
- ■ Highland
- ≡ Upland

World Climate Zones

South America, with a land area of approximately 6,883,000 square miles (17,826,970 kilometers), is the world's fourth-largest continent. Asia, Africa, and North America are larger. Shaped rather like a pork chop, South America is widest in the north and tapers to a point at its southern end. The greatest north-south distance is 4,750 miles (7,644 kilometers) and the greatest east-west distance is 3,200 miles

▲ **Above:** *South America's climate is similar to that of central and southern Africa.*

◄◄ **Opposite:** *Among South America's most striking topographical features are the Andes Mountains, which run almost the entire length of the continent.*

11

(5,150 kilometers), which is the distance from the northwest coast of Peru to the easternmost point on the coast of Brazil.

South America is completely surrounded by water, except for the isthmus of Panama, which connects Colombia to Central America. (An isthmus is a narrow strip of land that connects two land masses.) The Caribbean Sea is to the north, the Atlantic Ocean lies to the northeast and east, and the Pacific Ocean is to the west. Cape Horn, at the southern tip of South America, lies only about 600 miles (966 kilometers) from Antarctica. As you can see from the map on page 10, Bolivia and Paraguay are the only two countries in South America that do not touch water.

To learn about what South America is like, you might start by referring to maps that show its physical features (topography), its climate, land use, and other natural characteristics.

The Topography of South America

South America has three main geographic regions: the Andes Mountains, the Highlands, and the Central Plains. The Andes Mountains are easy to spot on the physical map on page 10. They are the world's longest mountain range above sea level. The mountains run along the western length of South America from Venezuela in the north, south to Tierra del Fuego—the large island at the southern tip of the continent. This is a young mountain chain, much like the Rockies in North America and the Alps in Europe. The Andes consist of high, jagged peaks broken by broad plateaus and deep valleys.

Aconcagua, an Andean peak in Argentina, is the highest point in South America and the tallest mountain in the Western Hemisphere. It rises to 23,034 feet (7,021 meters) above sea level. That is about 6,000 feet (1,829 meters) lower than Mt. Everest—the highest mountain in the Eastern Hemisphere and the world. However, South America has the distinction of having the highest navigable lake in the world, Lake Titicaca. This lake lies in the Andes on the border

between Bolivia and Peru, at a height of 12,507 feet (3,812 meters). South America is also home to the world's highest waterfall. Angel Falls, in eastern Venezuela, drops 3,212 feet (979 meters).

In the eastern part of South America, older mountains make up the Highlands area. Since older mountains have had more time to erode, these are lower than the Andes. There are two main Highlands regions: The Guiana Highlands in the northeast and the Brazilian Highlands in the east.

Between the Andes and the Highlands, and stretching the length of the continent, lie the Central Plains. This is where the great river systems of South America are located. The largest of these is the Amazon system. The Amazon River originates in the Peruvian Andes and empties into the Atlantic Ocean, off the coast of Brazil. The Amazon is the second-longest river in the world; only the Nile is longer. However, the Amazon carries the most water of any river in the world because of the large number of rivers that feed into it. The Amazon is at the heart of the world's largest rain forest.

Other major South American river systems include the Rio de la Plata and the Orinoco Rivers. The Orinoco makes up part of the Colombia-Venezuela border, then flows eastward across the middle of

Venezuela to empty into the Atlantic Ocean. In the Orinoco River basin area of Venezuela you'll find rolling grassland that provides grazing for large numbers of cattle.

In northern Argentina, the Rio de la Plata river system empties into a bay near Buenos Aires. This system includes the Paraná, Paraguay, and Uruguay Rivers. The Itaipu Dam, a hydroelectric dam on the Paraná River between Paraguay and Brazil, is the world's most powerful hydroelectric plant.

A treeless, fertile, grassy plain called the Pampa covers central Argentina. Drier, rockier grassland covers the plateau of southern Argentina, which is called Patagonia.

Climate and Weather

Climate and weather are not the same thing. Weather is short-lived; it changes from day to day. Climate is the average characteristics of the weather in a given place over a long period of time. Although climates can change, they do so much more slowly than weather— over many years, rather than days.

Meteorologists use a variety of high-tech methods to gather the information that allows them to analyze and predict the weather. Among those methods are sophisticated ways of viewing and mapping the world.

Analyzing and Predicting Weather

The major elements that are used to describe the weather and categorize climate are: temperature, precipitation, humidity, amount of sunshine, wind, and air pressure.

Manned and unmanned weather stations on land and at sea, weather balloons, airplanes, and satellites are all used in gathering weather information for analysis. Radar, cameras, and thermal infrared sensors monitor and record the weather conditions.

The information from these sources is sent to weather centers throughout the world by means of a worldwide satellite system, called the Global Telecommunications System (GTS). The information is fed into computers that record and analyze the data, which can then be compiled into highly detailed and informative maps. The GTS also allows weather centers to share their data.

By studying global weather patterns over a long time, climatologists can map climatic regions—areas that have similar climates. The world climate zones map on page 11 is just one example of this kind of map.

South America's Climate

South America's climate is generally warm, with wide variations in rainfall. Ocean winds and currents, and the barrier created by the Andes Mountains all determine the continent's pattern of rainfall. The climate map on page 16 illustrates the major climate regions of South America.

- The tropical wet climate, indicated by dark green, is where you'll find the rain forest. The huge tropical rain forest of the Amazon River basin is in northeastern Brazil. It is about 2 million square miles (5,180,000 square kilometers). Areas with a tropical wet climate are hot, averaging 80 degrees Fahrenheit year-round (27 degrees Celsius). Rainfall is consistently heavy throughout the year.
- A tropical dry climate (lighter green) is typical of most of the rest of northern South America. These areas are also hot, but they have both wet and dry seasons.
- Southern Brazil, Paraguay, Uruguay, and northeastern Argentina have a humid sub-tropical climate (lime green). This climate is marked by warm to hot summers averaging 80 degrees Fahrenheit (27 degrees Celsius), cool winters averaging 50 degrees Fahrenheit (10 degrees Celsius), and moderate precipitation all year.
- The southern part of Chile has a marine west coast climate. For the most part, this mild climate—colored blue-green on the map—features temperatures that do not vary much from season to season. Temperatures are generally around 70 degrees Fahrenheit (21 degrees

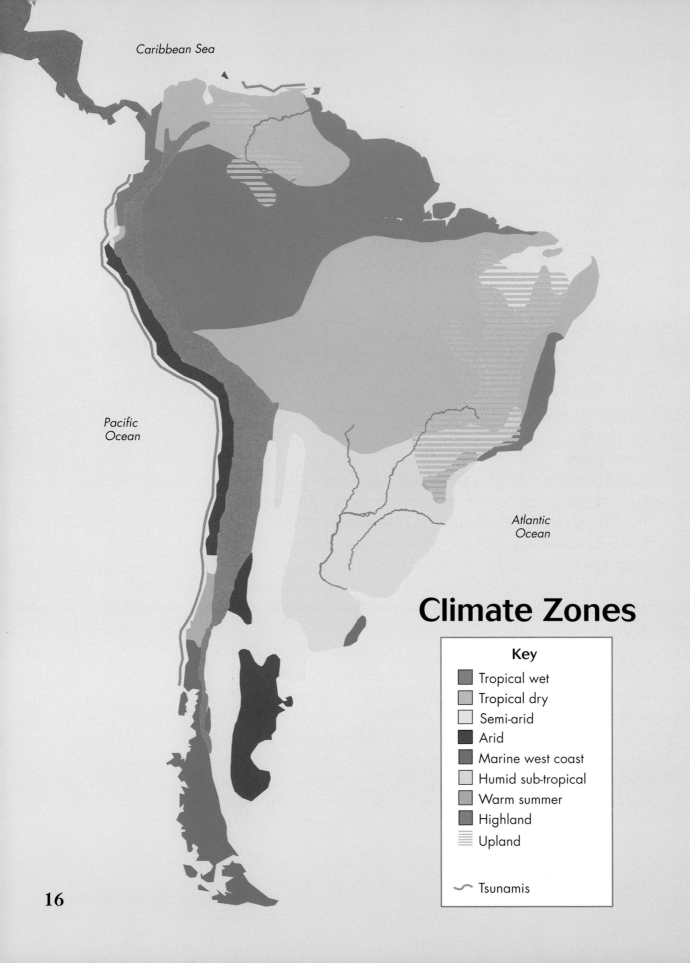

Caribbean Sea

Pacific
Ocean

Atlantic
Ocean

Climate Zones

Key	
	Tropical wet
	Tropical dry
	Semi-arid
	Arid
	Marine west coast
	Humid sub-tropical
	Warm summer
	Highland
	Upland
	Tsunamis

Celsius) in summer and 55 degrees Fahrenheit (13 degrees Celsius) in winter. Precipitation is slightly heavier than it is in humid subtropical regions. However, the climate in Tierra del Fuego, at the southernmost tip of South America, is not especially welcoming. Although temperatures rarely drop below freezing in the winter, summer temperatures rarely get above 49 degrees Fahrenheit (9 degrees Celsius). In addition, strong winds often howl across the land, and it is constantly cloudy and stormy. Since there are glaciers in this part of the world, the name *Tierra del Fuego*, which means "Land of Fire" in Spanish, is not especially fitting. The name was given to this area by the explorer Ferdinand Magellan in the 1500s. While he was sailing in this area, he spotted the fires that natives built on the beaches to keep warm.

- Pockets of land with semi-arid climate zones (colored gold), characterized by light, irregular precipitation, can be found on the northern tip of Colombia, the north coast of Venezuela, northeastern Brazil, and southern Argentina. The coast of Peru, northern Chile, and southeastern Argentina are even drier. These arid (pink) areas include deserts, where there is very little precipitation at any time. In fact, the Atacama Desert in northern Chile is one of the driest places on earth. The town of Arica, near the border of Peru, has the world's lowest average annual rainfall: .03 inch (.08 centimeter).

- Highland areas, colored brown on the map, are found along the Andes range. These high-altitude areas are consistently cold, and the tallest peaks are snow-covered year-round.

- Areas where an elevated topography tends to moderate the climate of the immediate surrounding area have an upland climate (shown in brown stripes). The climate is different in degree, not type. Depending on the actual elevation, its effect is sometimes so slight that it is hard to detect. The upland areas indicated on the opposite page tend to be somewhat cooler and drier than surrounding regions.

◄◄ *Opposite: The Amazon rain forest is in the tropical wet zone in the north.*

Animals and Plants

South America's hot, humid rain forests are home to a rich variety of South American animals. Jaguars stalk the forest floor at night and bats hang overhead during the day. The calls of hundreds of colorful birds—including parrots, hummingbirds, toucans, and macaws—fill the air. Below, insects of all sizes scurry through the forest growth. Lively capuchin and spider monkeys leap overhead, while sloths make their slow, upside-down progress through the trees. The capybara, the world's largest rodent at 4 feet (1 meter) long, is found in the rain forest, as are lizards, alligators, and many colorful frogs and toads. Sharp-toothed piranha fish flash through the rivers while anacondas—one of the largest constrictor snakes—slide by on land as well as in the water.

▼ *Below: Although most vicuñas are wild, this Bolivian boy has a vicuña on a lead.*

The heat and rainfall of the Amazon rain forest also provide perfect conditions for thousands of plants—more than in any other place in the world. Fine furniture is made from rain forest hardwood trees such as mahogany and rosewood. Brazil-nut and rubber trees also grow there. Beautiful orchids stand out among the greenery, and climbing plants and vines wind their way toward the light from the forest floor. South of this region, in northern Argentina and southern Bolivia, the rain forest gives way to forests of quebracho trees. Tannin, which is used for tanning leather, is a product of the quebracho.

Long-haired anteaters, sturdy armadillos, and the rhea—a large, flightless bird similar to the ostrich—roam the dry grasslands of the Pampa in Uruguay and central Argentina. The maned wolf makes its home here as well, stalking its prey on tall, skinny legs.

In the Andes, you will find four members of the camel family. Guanacos and vicuñas live in the wild,

making their way along steep mountain trails, while llamas and alpacas have been domesticated. The wool from both the vicuñas and the alpacas is sheared for human wear, although regulations have been placed against hunting the dwindling population of vicuñas.

Another resident of the Andes is the spectacled bear, the only bear in South America. Chinchillas and guinea pigs are two of the smaller residents of the mountains. Soaring high above is the Andean condor, with the wingspan of 10 feet (3 meters).

South America's deserts provide a home for burrowing rodents, insects, cacti, and flowering plants that bloom during brief rainy periods. The Atacama Desert in northern Chile and the Sechura Desert in northern Peru are so dry, however, that they are almost totally bare of animals and plants except in areas that have been artificially irrigated.

▲ **Above:** *This poison-dart frog is one of the many poisonous frogs that live in the South American rain forests.*

How Climate and Topography Affect People

As we have seen, climate greatly affects plant and animal life. Of course, a region's climate and topography can affect many aspects of human life as well. Among them:

Population distribution. More people tend to settle in areas that have a mild or moderate climate, adequate rainfall, and fairly level, open land. Population will be less densely distributed in regions that are mountainous or thickly forested, and in regions with climates that are very cold or dry. You can see this connection if you compare the world climate zones map on page 11 in this chapter with the world population density map on page 33 in Chapter 2.

How people live and work. The type of housing people live in, the clothes they wear, and the kind of work they do, all depend in part on the climate of their region. The physical structure of the land also can affect what work people do. For example, large-scale farming is an option in the plains areas, but not in mountain regions.

Agriculture. To a large extent, climate dictates what crops can or can't be successfully grown in an area. Using technology, such as artificial irrigation or greenhouses, can change the impact of weather and climate to a degree. However, agriculture is most successful when crops are naturally suited to the area in which they are grown.

Transportation. An area's climate and topography can dictate which forms of transportation are used there. For example, dogsleds are an obvious choice in arctic areas, while camels or elephants are well suited to travel in hot, arid conditions. More roads and railroads will be built in areas that have a level terrain, as opposed to mountainous areas.

Economy. Some areas, such as deserts, have little or no natural resources. These areas have a climate or topography that doesn't allow for extensive agriculture or a developed transportation system. Such harsh regions will probably be poorer than areas that can support industry, large-scale agriculture, or other means of making a living and engaging in trade.

South America: The Land and Its People

The native peoples of the Amazon have adapted their lifestyle to suit the land. Where they farm, they clear small plots of land by the slash-and-burn method—cutting down trees and burning them to provide ashes for fertilizer. These small plots are easier to work by hand, and they are protected from direct rainfall, which would wash away the thin soil. When the soil does begin to wear out, the Amazon people move to a new area and let the first place grow wild again before returning. This style of farming, called "shifting agriculture," protects the land by allowing it to renew its fertility naturally.

When the Amazon people hunt and fish, they use bows and arrows, blowguns, spears, and poisons taken from animals and plants. Houses are made of wood and thatch, sleeping hammocks are woven from plant fibers, and cooking pots and other containers are sculpted from river clay. Natural plant dyes are used for decoration; seeds, clay beads, and feathers are used to make jewelry and ceremonial headdresses.

Most Amazon groups have had at least some contact with people from the "outside," and many have begun to adopt a more modern lifestyle. Others are working hard to maintain their traditional ways, to live *with* the land rather than on it.

The Land of South America and the Economy

South American lands are a valuable resource for mining minerals, growing crops, and grazing farm animals. Single-product plantations and huge ranches are the main sources of agricultural income. By looking at the grazing land on the land use map, you can see that the majority of the usable land is given over to livestock.

Crops

One of South America's most important crops is coffee. Brazil is the world's leading producer, supplying about one fourth of the world's coffee. Colombia ranks second in coffee production.

Corn and wheat are especially suited to areas such as the Andean region and central Argentina, where the climate is cool or dry. Sugarcane, cotton, and bananas, on the other hand, are important crops in warm, tropical areas such as Guyana, Paraguay, and coastal Brazil and Venezuela. Rice is found primarily in the warm, lowland, coastal areas of Colombia and in southeastern Brazil. Other important Brazilian products include oranges, which Brazil exports as orange juice concentrate, and cacao. Cacao comes from the seeds of an evergreen tree and is the source of chocolate and cocoa. In addition, grapes grown in Argentine and Chilean vineyards contribute to a thriving South American wine industry.

Coca, a native plant, is grown in South America for the production of cocaine, which is illegal, but also very profitable. Colombia is one the world's largest suppliers to the international illegal drug trade.

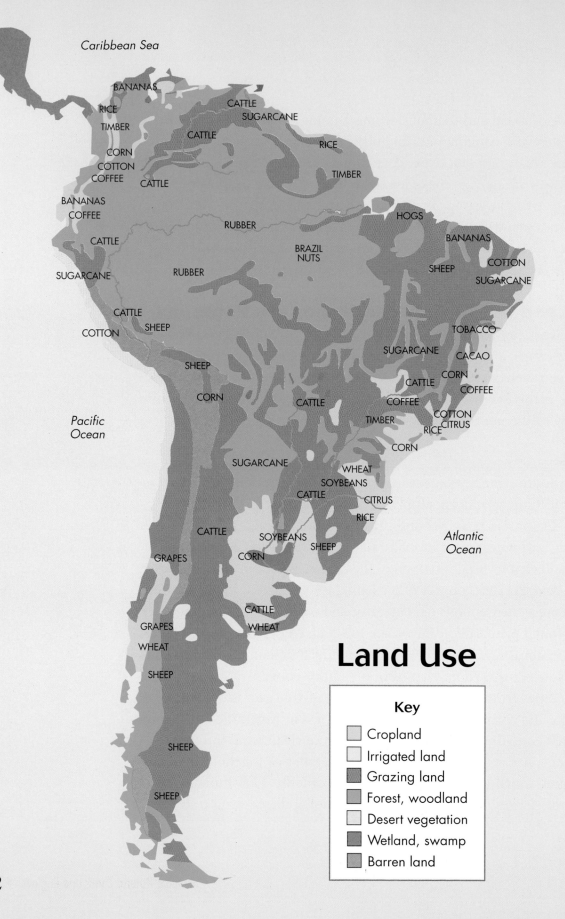

Caribbean Sea

BANANAS
RICE
TIMBER
CORN
COTTON
COFFEE
CATTLE

CATTLE
SUGARCANE
CATTLE

RICE

TIMBER

BANANAS
COFFEE
CATTLE

SUGARCANE

CATTLE
COTTON
SHEEP

SHEEP

CORN

RUBBER

RUBBER

BRAZIL
NUTS

HOGS

BANANAS
COTTON
SUGARCANE

SHEEP

TOBACCO
CACAO
CORN
COFFEE
COTTON
CITRUS

SUGARCANE

CATTLE
COFFEE
TIMBER
RICE
CORN

Pacific
Ocean

SUGARCANE

CATTLE

WHEAT
SOYBEANS
CATTLE
CITRUS
RICE

Atlantic
Ocean

CATTLE

GRAPES
CORN

SOYBEANS
SHEEP

GRAPES

CATTLE
WHEAT

WHEAT

SHEEP

SHEEP

SHEEP

Land Use

Key
- ▢ Cropland
- ▢ Irrigated land
- ▢ Grazing land
- ▢ Forest, woodland
- ▢ Desert vegetation
- ▢ Wetland, swamp
- ▢ Barren land

Livestock

Cattle and sheep are the main commercial livestock raised in South America. While cattle ranches are found throughout the continent, the biggest and most important are located in the Pampa in central Argentina. There, cattle graze on ranches that sometimes cover hundreds of thousands of acres. Other large cattle ranches are found in Brazil and Venezuela. The greatest concentration of sheep is found in southern Argentina, on the cool, dry hills of Patagonia.

Forestry

The majority of South America's forests are located in Brazil, where in the Amazon rain forest, hardwoods such as mahogany are cut for the manufacture of fine furniture, rubber trees are tapped for their sap, and Brazil nuts are harvested. Elsewhere in Brazil, as well as in Paraguay and southern Chile, you'll find wood used by the construction, paper, and leather-tanning industries. Most South American timber, however, is used for fuel.

Mineral Resources

South America contains a number of important minerals, distributed unevenly throughout the continent. Look at the mineral resources map on page 24. As you can see, most of the mineral wealth lies near the coastline. The main exceptions are Bolivia and part of Brazil's Amazon River basin.

Copper is mined extensively in Chile and Peru, and copper deposits are also found in Brazil. Bolivia is a leading world producer of tin; Peru and Brazil have less important deposits.

Brazil and Venezuela are the primary producers of iron ore, while Bolivia and Peru have lead and zinc mines. Bauxite, which is used to make aluminum, is an important resource in Brazil, Suriname, and Guyana. Major tungsten mines can be found in Brazil, Bolivia, and Peru, and smaller mines are in Argentina. Tungsten is a metal that is used inside of light bulbs.

◀◀ *Opposite: Coffee is one of South America's most important export crops.*

Caribbean Sea

Pacific
Ocean

Atlantic
Ocean

Mineral
Resources

Key	
■	Coal
○	Petroleum
▲	Iron ore
◆	Tin
▨	Copper
△	Zinc
✖	Tungsten
✚	Lead
◗	Bauxite
▽	Sulfur

Coal is mined in various areas of South America, as you can see from the map. However, the deposits are not extensive and, with the exception of Colombia's coal, most of the coal is low-grade.

Energy Production and Consumption

A look at the energy production map on page 26 shows that South America's principal energy resources are oil and natural gas. These resources are found primarily in the northwest and along the southern half of the Andes Mountain chain.

By comparing the political (page 32) and energy production maps, you can easily see which countries produce the most energy. Venezuela's extensive oil reserves make that country the leading petroleum producer in South America and a major world producer. Other valuable oil fields and basins are found in Colombia, Argentina, Ecuador, and along the eastern coast of Brazil. Extensive natural gas deposits are found in eastern Bolivia, Argentina, and Colombia.

The energy consumption map on page 27 shows that Argentina, Venezuela, and Suriname consume the most energy. Venezuela's oil production and refining and Suriname's bauxite mining and aluminum production consume a great deal of energy. Argentina is one of South America's most industrialized countries. Compared with most South American countries, Argentina seems to consume huge amounts of energy. However, you need to be careful when reading this map.

For instance, what about Brazil, the most industrialized country in South America? Doesn't Brazil consume a lot of energy, too? Look again at the map key. Notice that the map shows "consumption per capita" (per person). As a country, Brazil consumes a lot of energy. However, approximately five times more people live in Brazil than in Argentina. When Brazil's total energy consumption is divided among all the people in the country, each person's consumption—the per capita amount—is relatively small compared to the per capita energy consumption in Argentina, which has a much smaller population.

◀◀ *Opposite: Most of South America's mineral deposits are near the coast.*

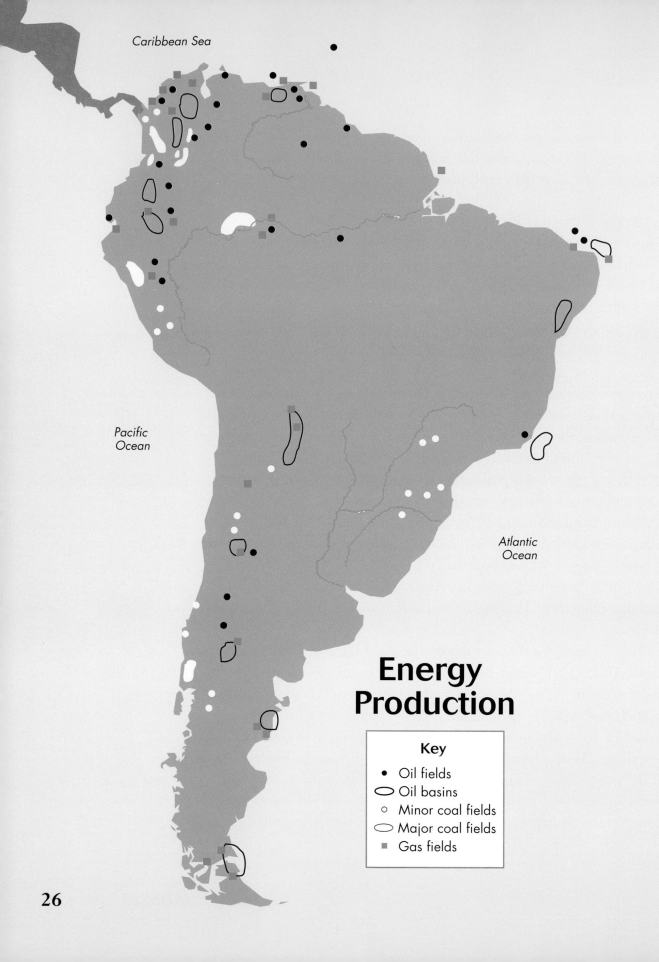

Caribbean Sea

Pacific
Ocean

Atlantic
Ocean

Energy
Production

Key
● Oil fields
⬭ Oil basins
∘ Minor coal fields
⬯ Major coal fields
■ Gas fields

Think of dividing one large pizza evenly among your classmates, or dividing that same size pizza evenly among your family. Fewer people means a bigger slice!

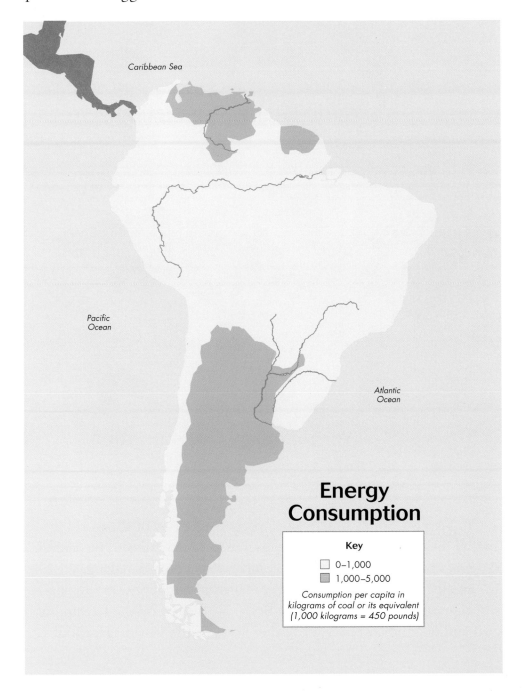

Caribbean Sea

Pacific
Ocean

Atlantic
Ocean

Energy Consumption

Key	
☐	0–1,000
▨	1,000–5,000

Consumption per capita in kilograms of coal or its equivalent (1,000 kilograms = 450 pounds)

◀ **Left:** *Venezuela's oil refineries contribute to its high energy consumption.*

◀◀ **Opposite:** *Most of South America's gas and oil fields are in the northern and western parts of the continent.*

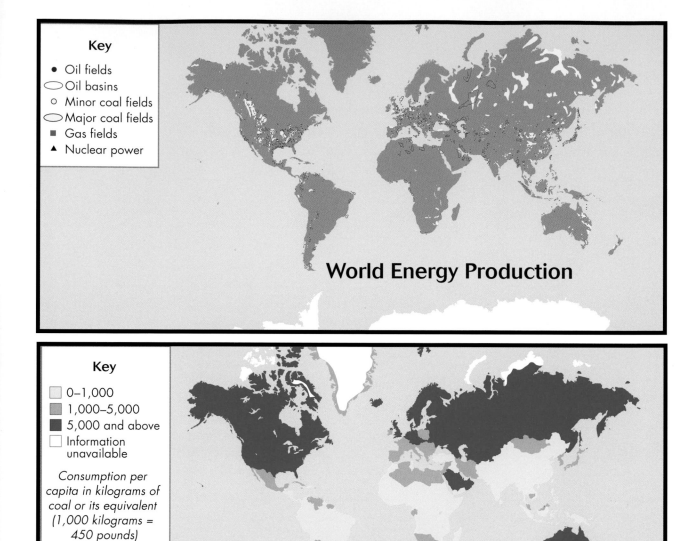

Key

- • Oil fields
- ⬭ Oil basins
- ○ Minor coal fields
- ⬭ Major coal fields
- ▪ Gas fields
- ▲ Nuclear power

World Energy Production

Key

- ☐ 0–1,000
- ▨ 1,000–5,000
- ■ 5,000 and above
- ☐ Information unavailable

Consumption per capita in kilograms of coal or its equivalent (1,000 kilograms = 450 pounds)

World Energy Consumption

▲ *Above:* Among the world's continents, South America is a light producer and consumer of energy.

To see how South America compares to the rest of the world in energy production and consumption, see the maps above. Be careful, though, that you understand the comparisons you are making.

Finally, take a look at the map of harmful emissions on the opposite page. Here you can see how Brazil is affected by the burning of coal and oil, and compare it to other areas of the world. Harmful emissions from the burning of fossil fuels contribute to environmental problems such as global warming, destruction of the ozone layer, and acid rain. South America produces fewer emissions than Europe, Asia, or North America, but more than Africa and Australia.

The Environment

South America's environmental problems are shown on the environmental damage map on page 30. Acid rain is a particular problem in the highly industrialized areas of the north and along the center of the east coast. The gases in the atmosphere that produce acid rain come mainly from burning coal, oil, and gas for fuel or in factories. Acid rain weakens and destroys trees and plants and also pollutes water, killing any fish that live there.

The points of human-induced salinization are areas where intensive irrigation has washed the nutrients from the soil, leaving it encrusted with salts. Salinized land is unsuitable for raising crops or grazing livestock.

▼ *Below: South America contributes a relatively small amount of fossil fuels to Earth's atmosphere.*

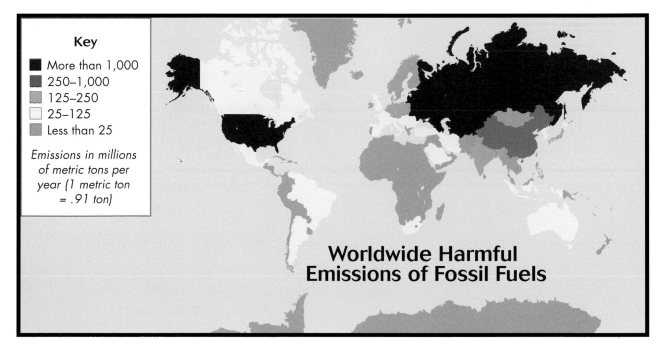

Key

- ■ More than 1,000
- ■ 250–1,000
- ■ 125–250
- □ 25–125
- ■ Less than 25

Emissions in millions of metric tons per year (1 metric ton = .91 ton)

Worldwide Harmful Emissions of Fossil Fuels

Caribbean Sea

Pacific
Ocean

Caracas

Bogotá

Quito

Atlantic
Ocean

São Paulo

Rio de Janeiro

Mendoza

Santiago

Santa Fe

La Plata

Environmental
Damage

Key

- Human-induced desertification
- Tropical deforestation
- Tropical forest remaining
- Coastal pollution
- Human-induced salinization
- Area affected by acid rain
- Selected city with high level of air pollution

Desertification can result from either overgrazing or efforts to increase agricultural production. Intensive farming methods, including the increased use of chemicals, deplete the soil. By comparing the land use map on page 22 with the environmental damage map, you can see that overgrazing is the major factor at work in South America. However, as the salinization points show, intensive farming plays a part in desertification as well.

South America's coastal pollution is caused by several factors, including shipping, factory waste, and, in Peru, agricultural waste from increased use of chemical fertilizers. Population pressure plays a part in coastal pollution, too, especially along South America's east coast. Compare the environmental damage map and major cities map (page 34) to see this connection.

The problem of deforestation is a major concern in South America. Although the map shows that a relatively small portion of the tropical rain forest has been destroyed, this is deceptive. The destruction of the rain forest is continuous. In the past 50 years, Colombia, for example, has lost nearly 50 percent of its forest. Logging, mining, and burning the forest to provide land for agriculture continue to contribute to the disappearance of the world's largest rain forest. Logging alone accounts for the loss of 50 million acres (20 million hectares) each year.

A Closer Look

You can learn a lot about what a place is like by looking at different kinds of maps, one at a time. However, by comparing the information presented in two or more maps, you can discover something about how and why it got that way.

Compare the climate and land use maps from this chapter. How does the climate map explain the way South America's land is used? Now compare the climate map (page 16) and the population density map in Chapter 2 on page 46. What conclusions can you make about why people live where they do?

◄◄ *Opposite:*
Overgrazing of farm animals is a major cause of the desertification that affects much of South America.

Caribbean Sea

VENEZUELA

GUYANA

SURINAME

FRENCH GUIANA

COLOMBIA

ECUADOR

PERU

BRAZIL

BOLIVIA

Pacific
Ocean

CHILE

PARAGUAY

Atlantic
Ocean

URUGUAY

ARGENTINA

Political Map

Scale		
1,000 km		
1,000 mi.		

FALKLAND
ISLANDS

Mapping People, Cultures, and the Political World

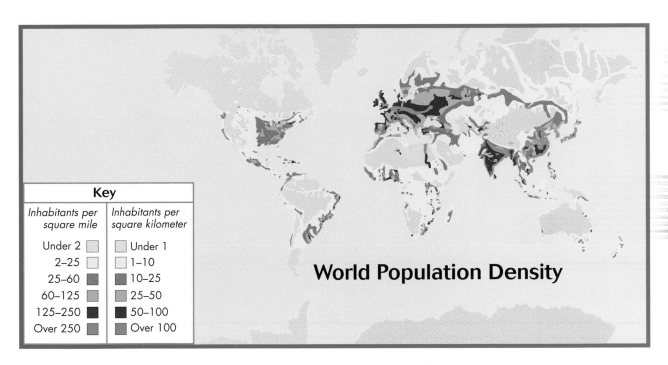

Key	
Inhabitants per square mile	*Inhabitants per square kilometer*
Under 2	Under 1
2–25	1–10
25–60	10–25
60–125	25–50
125–250	50–100
Over 250	Over 100

World Population Density

Maps can reveal much more about a place than simply what it is like physically. They can also tell you a great deal about the political divisions of the area. Maps can inform you about the cultures and customs of the people who live there as well. They can show the languages spoken in a region, the religions people identify with, and the places where most people live.

▲ *Above:* South America's densest population pockets are near the coast, just as they are in Africa.

◄◄ *Opposite:* The map face of South America has not changed much in the last 100 years.

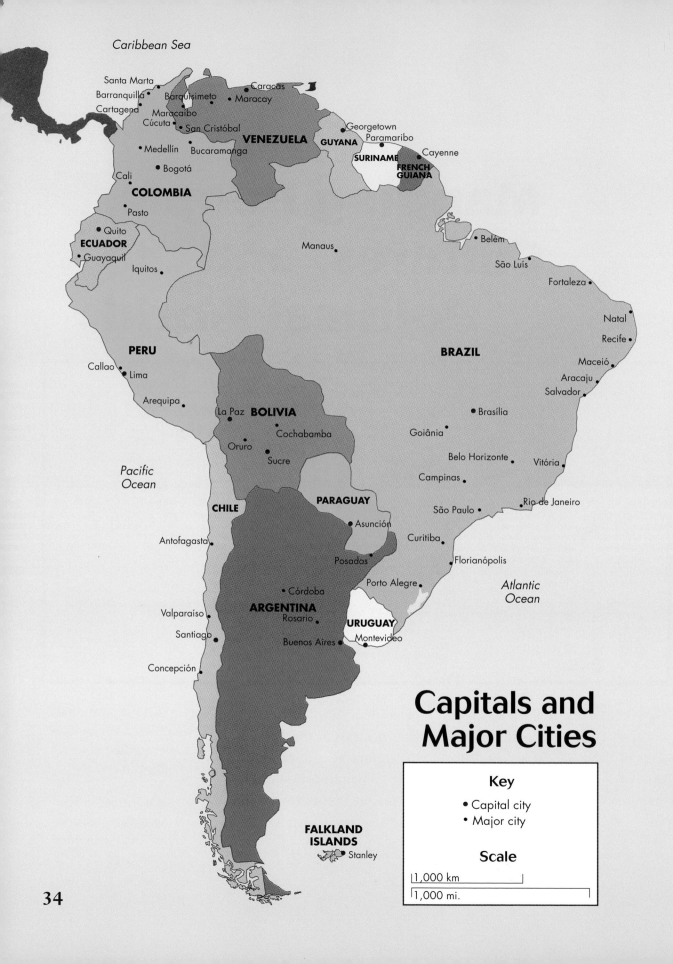

Caribbean Sea

Santa Marta
Barranquilla
Cartagena

Caracas
Maracay
Barquisimeto
Maracaibo
Cúcuta
San Cristóbal
VENEZUELA

Georgetown
Paramaribo
GUYANA
SURINAME
Cayenne
FRENCH GUIANA

Medellín
Bucaramanga

Cali
Bogotá
COLOMBIA

Pasto

Quito
ECUADOR
Guayaquil

Iquitos

Manaus

Belém
São Luís
Fortaleza

Natal
Recife

PERU

Callao
Lima

Arequipa

La Paz
BOLIVIA
Cochabamba
Oruro
Sucre

BRAZIL

Maceió
Aracaju
Salvador

Brasília

Goiânia

Belo Horizonte
Vitória
Campinas

Pacific Ocean

CHILE

PARAGUAY
Asunción

São Paulo
Rio de Janeiro

Curitiba

Posadas

Florianópolis

Antofagasta

Córdoba

Porto Alegre
Atlantic Ocean

ARGENTINA
Rosario

Valparaíso

Santiago
Buenos Aires
URUGUAY
Montevideo

Concepción

Capitals and Major Cities

FALKLAND ISLANDS
Stanley

Key
• Capital city
• Major city

Scale

1,000 km

1,000 mi.

34

The Political World: Dividing the Land

Political maps such as the one on page 32 are familiar to everyone. In these, there is no attempt to show what an area physically looks like. Rather, a political map shows the boundaries that separate countries (or states and provinces). Colors are used to distinguish one country from another. A political map may also show capitals and major cities, as the map on the opposite page does.

Boundaries are artificial; that is, they are created, set, and changed by people. Conquests, wars, and treaties have all caused boundary changes. Political maps can, therefore, also be a guide to the history of a region.

Geographers keep track of boundary changes, and country and city name changes, as they occur, so that new, up-to-date political maps can be created as soon as possible.

Nature's Influence

The political world is not entirely separate from the natural world. Rivers or mountains may dictate where boundaries are set. Also, if there is a wealth of natural resources in one location, people may try to set boundaries that put all or most of those resources within their own country's borders. Cities, too, are often located according to natural features. Comparing climate and major city maps will show that cities tend to cluster along coastlines or major waterways, and in areas that have less severe climates.

South America's History and Political Divisions

From the time of pre-Colombian native civilizations through the period when Europeans established colonies in South America, the continent's history has been shaped by a desire to exploit South America's natural resources.

Native Cultures

Native people inhabited South America long before Europeans knew the continent existed. By 6,000 B.C., various groups lived throughout

◀◀ *Opposite:* Given its size, Argentina has relatively few large cities.

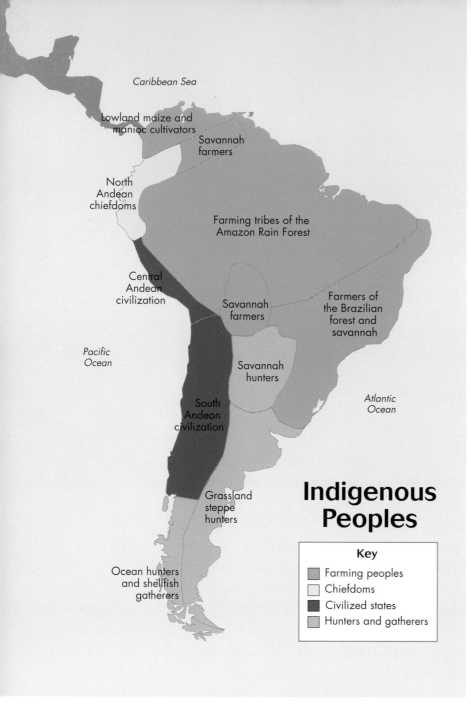

Caribbean Sea

Lowland maize and
manioc cultivators

Savannah
farmers

North
Andean
chiefdoms

Farming tribes of the
Amazon Rain Forest

Central
Andean
civilization

Savannah
farmers

Farmers of
the Brazilian
forest and
savannah

Pacific
Ocean

Savannah
hunters

South
Andean
civilization

Atlantic
Ocean

Grassland
steppe
hunters

Indigenous
Peoples

Ocean hunters
and shellfish
gatherers

Key	
⬜	Farming peoples
⬜	Chiefdoms
⬛	Civilized states
⬜	Hunters and gatherers

▲ *Above:* Many of South
America's early societies
farmed the land.

South America. In some regions, nomadic lifestyles gave way to a settled existence. In the Andes, great civilizations evolved.

Look at the indigenous peoples map on this page. Here you can see the lifestyles of the continent's early cultures. Farming societies based on the cultivation of maize (a type of corn) were first established in the north. Gradually these peoples spread southward. They adapted farming to the hot, humid areas of the rain forest, to the drier forests of southeastern Brazil, and to the eastern and central grasslands.

The south-central and southern areas of the continent had soil that was poorly suited to farming. The native groups in these areas relied on hunting and gathering for their food. Because there were few animals to hunt—the guanaco and rhea were the primary food sources—the people in these areas led a much less settled existence than northern groups. At the far southwestern tip of the continent, the primary food source was—and still is—the animals of the ocean and shore, including fish, shellfish, birds, and seals.

Advanced civilizations thrived in the Andes. In the early 1400s the Inca, operating from their capital city of Cuzco in southern Peru, began to overthrow the other Andean societies. The Inca Empire eventually stretched from southern Colombia to central Chile and included what are now Ecuador, Peru, northern Chile, western Bolivia, and northwestern Argentina. The Inca built cities out of stone, and they developed irrigation systems and terraced the land for farming. They crafted beautiful objects out of gold and silver.

▲◄ *Above left:* This gold mask was probably made by an Inca metalworker.

▲► *Above right:* The famed Machu Picchu, in Peru, is the ruins of an Inca city.

European Exploration

Soon after Christopher Columbus reached the New World in 1492, Spain and Portugal began the exploration of South America. In an attempt to fairly divide the new lands, the two countries signed the Treaty of Tordesillas in 1494. This established the Line of Demarcation—an imaginary north-south line. Portugal could settle all lands east of the line, which included only the "bulge"—the easternmost third of present-day Brazil. Spain could settle all of the lands west of the line.

In 1500, the Portuguese explorer Pedro Alvares Cabral reached the east coast of Brazil and officially claimed the land for Portugal. Twenty years later, Ferdinand Magellan found the route from the Atlantic to the Pacific around the southern tip of South America between the mainland and Tierra del Fuego. In recognition of his feat, the southernmost area of South America was called Magellanica on the maps of the time. Today, the narrow waterway on which Magellan sailed is known as the Strait of Magellan.

In 1532, Spanish conquerors, led by Francisco Pizzaro, arrived on the west coast of South America and began to overthrow the Inca Empire.

Colonial South America

Despite the Line of Demarcation, countries other than Spain and Portugal established settlements in South America. Dutch, British, and French settlers fought for land on the northern coast.

Although Portugal was supposed to settle only the area east of the Line of Demarcation, Brazilian-born Portuguese *bandeirantes* (pathfinders) explored and settled vast areas west of the line during the late 1500s and early 1600s. At that time, the coastal areas of South America were well mapped. But there were no accurate maps of the interior of the continent, particularly of the Amazon rain forest region, until the 1700s and 1800s. During that period, many scientific societies sent individuals and expeditions to South America. Naturalists such as Alexander von Humboldt spent years exploring, drawing, and mapping the distribution of plants, animals, and geographic features of this new world.

By the late 1700s, four European countries controlled South America. As you can see from the map on page 39, the Netherlands and France divided Guiana, Portugal controlled Brazil, and Spain ruled the rest of the continent. Spanish South America was divided into three jurisdictions: the Viceroyalty (colony) of New Granada, the Viceroyalty of Peru, and the Viceroyalty of La Plata.

During the colonial years, South America was heavily exploited for its resources. Agricultural products such as sugarcane and coffee and mineral products such as gold and silver were of major importance to the economies of Spain and Portugal. The colonies were expected to buy manufactured goods from Europe, and they were not encouraged to establish their own businesses.

These economic controls were unpopular with many South Americans, and so were the political controls exercised by the colonial powers in Europe. Criollos, (kree-OH-yohs), South American–born people of Spanish ancestry, and mestizos (meh-STEE-zohs), South Americans of mixed European and Indian ancestry, wanted a bigger say in how their countries were run. While Spain and Portugal were at war with France in the early 1800s, South Americans had their chance to break free of colonial rule.

Independence from Europe

From 1810 to 1825, a series of wars took place throughout Spanish South America. In 1811, the people of Paraguay overthrew Spanish rule in their country and declared independence. By the end of 1825, Spain's control over the rest of its South American colonies was broken with the help of two great South American heroes.

In the north, General Simon Bolívar, known as the "Great Liberator," helped free Venezuela, Colombia, Ecuador, Peru, and Bolivia from Spanish rule. In the south, General José Francisco de San Martín freed Argentina and Chile, and assisted Bolívar with fighting in Peru.

Brazil's ties to Portugal were cut peacefully, however, when the colony was declared an independent monarchy in 1822.

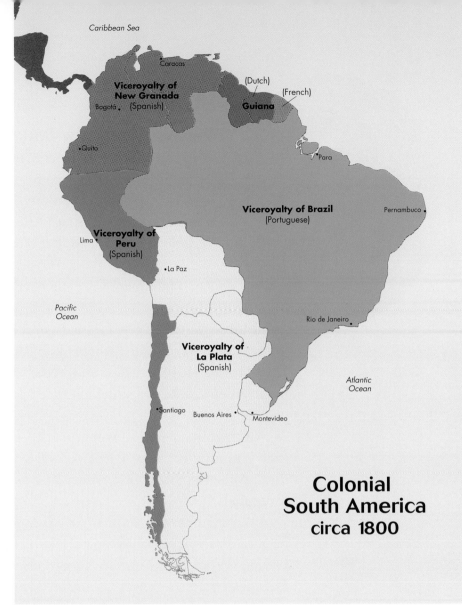

Caribbean Sea

Caracas

Viceroyalty of New Granada
(Spanish)

Bogotá

(Dutch)

(French)

Guiana

Quito

Para

Viceroyalty of Brazil
(Portuguese)

Pernambuco

Viceroyalty of Peru
(Spanish)

Lima

La Paz

Pacific Ocean

Rio de Janeiro

Viceroyalty of La Plata
(Spanish)

Atlantic Ocean

Santiago

Buenos Aires

Montevideo

Colonial South America circa 1800

▲ *Above: Most of South America was colonized by the Portuguese and the Spanish.*

Simon Bolívar

New Nations, New Boundaries

After the wars for independence from Europe, Venezuela, Ecuador, Guyana, Suriname, and Uruguay still did not exist as independent nations, and Bolivia extended to the southwest coast of South America.

Bolívar had hoped that one nation might be made of the different Spanish territories after they gained independence. His dream was only partly realized, however. In 1819, Bolívar formed the republic of Gran Colombia from the old Viceroyalty of New Granada, and he became its president. Gran Colombia included what is now Venezuela, Colombia, and Ecuador. In 1830, Ecuador and Venezuela broke away to become independent countries, at which time Gran Colombia became, simply, Colombia.

Meanwhile, in 1825, Argentina and Brazil began fighting over their common border. Three years later, in 1828, they signed a treaty that turned the disputed territory into the independent nation of Uruguay.

Look again at the colonial South America map. Notice the strip near La Paz where the Viceroyalty of La Plata connects to the Pacific Ocean. When South American nations won independence from European colonial powers, Bolivia controlled this area. Because the region was rich in nitrates (an important ingredient in fertilizer), Peru and Chile wanted to take the land from Bolivia. After a four-year war among the three countries (1879–1883), Chile won the right to this territory, plus a bit more. The end of the war established the present-day borders of Peru, Chile, and Bolivia. Almost 80 years later, in 1966, Guyana became independent. Suriname followed in 1975.

Population, Language, and Religion

Political maps tell us about the boundaries of a nation, but not about the lives of its inhabitants. Maps that focus on population, language, and religion tell us more about a country's people. Most countries'

Key

	Decrease
	0–1%
	1–2%
	2–3%
	>3%

(Does not include effects of migration)

World Annual Average Population Growth

governments conduct a census (population count) on some sort of regular basis. The United States, for example, has conducted a regular ten-year census since 1790.

Census figures are used to make maps that show how population is distributed. The world population density map on page 33 is one such map. By compiling statistics over a period of years—from census and birth and death records—geographers can make predictions regarding population growth, as shown in the map above.

Because many different languages may be spoken in any one country, it is difficult to map language distribution precisely. However, large areas that represent language families can be mapped, as shown in the world languages map on page 42. In the same way, predominant religions of an area can also be mapped, as shown in the world religions map on the same page.

South American Religions

A look at the map on page 43 shows that the vast majority of people in South America are Roman Catholic. This reflects the influence of the Spanish and Portuguese explorers and colonizers. They brought Catholicism to the continent and converted many of the native South Americans from their indigenous religions. Traditional native beliefs

▲ *Above: South America's population is expanding far more rapidly than those of the United States and Europe.*

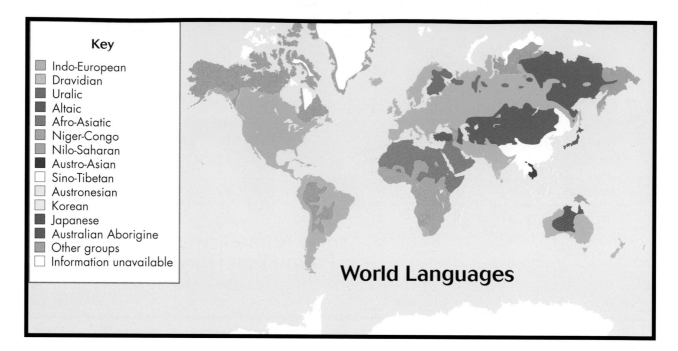

Key

- Indo-European
- Dravidian
- Uralic
- Altaic
- Afro-Asiatic
- Niger-Congo
- Nilo-Saharan
- Austro-Asian
- Sino-Tibetan
- Austronesian
- Korean
- Japanese
- Australian Aborigine
- Other groups
- Information unavailable

World Languages

▲▼ *Above and below:*
As these two maps demon-
strate, the population of
South America is more
homogeneous and less
diverse than the popula-
tions of Africa and Asia.

are often observed alongside or in combination with Catholic beliefs. In some areas, particularly in the Amazon region, indigenous religions are practiced exclusively.

The large Indian population of Guyana explains the importance of Hinduism in that country. Indians came to Guyana to work on plantations in the early 1800s, and now comprise a little more than half the country's population. The Indian population of Suriname is

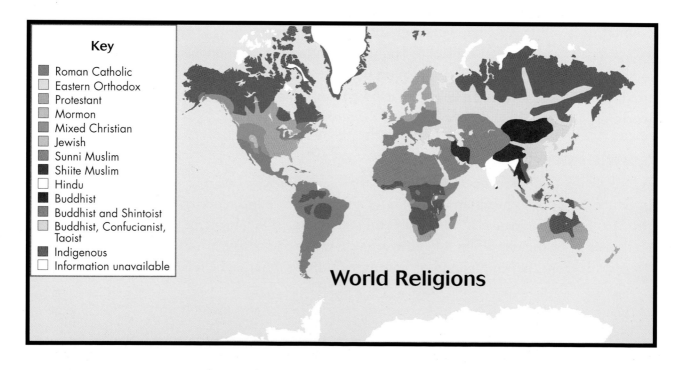

Key

- Roman Catholic
- Eastern Orthodox
- Protestant
- Mormon
- Mixed Christian
- Jewish
- Sunni Muslim
- Shiite Muslim
- Hindu
- Buddhist
- Buddhist and Shintoist
- Buddhist, Confucianist, Taoist
- Indigenous
- Information unavailable

World Religions

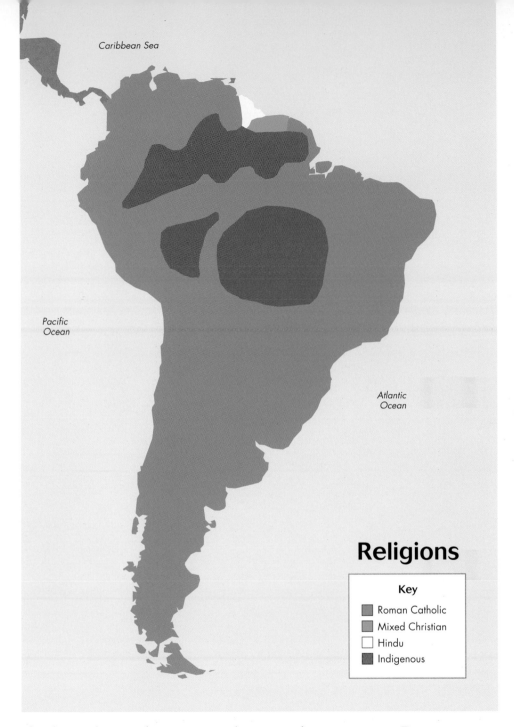

Caribbean Sea

Pacific
Ocean

Atlantic
Ocean

Religions

Key
- Roman Catholic
- Mixed Christian
- Hindu
- Indigenous

◀ *Left:* *The dominance of the Hindu religion (colored yellow) in Guyana reflects the many Asian Indians living in that country.*

also large, but in that country there are almost as many Protestants and Roman Catholics as there are Hindus. Each group makes up about 25 percent of the population. For that reason, Suriname is colored green, indicating that more than one Christian denomination predominates in the region.

Caribbean Sea

Pacific
Ocean

Atlantic
Ocean

Languages

Key

▢ Indo-European
▢ Other groups

▲ **Above:** *Although the Indo-European languages of Spanish and Portuguese are the main languages spoken in South America, many people speak native languages.*

South American Languages

As the languages map above shows, most South Americans speak Indo-European languages—primarily Spanish and, in Brazil, Portuguese. Approximately two thirds of South America's people speak Spanish. French is the official language of French Guiana, Dutch is the official language of Guyana, and English is the official language of Suriname.

The many different South American native cultures have their own languages. In some areas, marked in brown on the map, these languages are the primary ones spoken. Quechua, the language of the Inca, still predominates today among people living in the Andes, from southern Colombia to northern Argentina. In Peru, enough people speak Quechua that it is one of the official languages of that country. Another native language is Aymara, which is widely spoken in the La Paz area of Bolivia. Although many native people speak only their own language, particularly in remote areas, others often speak a mixture of their own language and their country's official language.

▼ **Below:** *The population in the northern part of South America is multiplying at a faster rate than the population in the southern part of the continent.*

South American Population Growth and Density

In 1996, South America had an estimated population of more than 323 million. The continent ranks fifth in total population, after Asia, Africa, Europe, and North America.

The population of South America is one of the fastest growing in the world. And, as you can see from the map this page, most of this growth is taking place in the northern half of the continent.

South America's population is unevenly distributed around the continent, as you

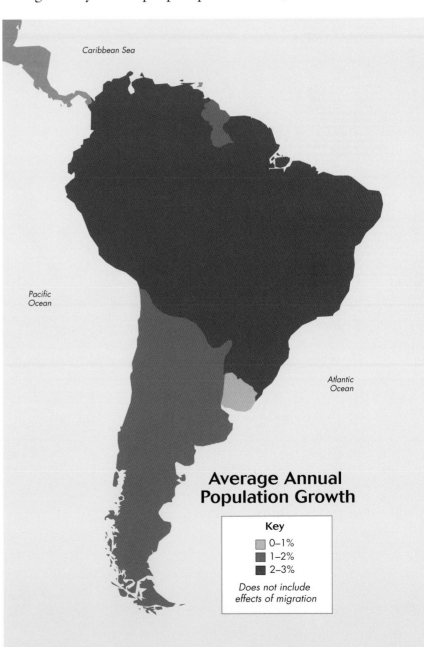

Caribbean Sea

Pacific Ocean

Atlantic Ocean

Average Annual Population Growth

Key
▢ 0–1%
▢ 1–2%
▢ 2–3%

Does not include effects of migration

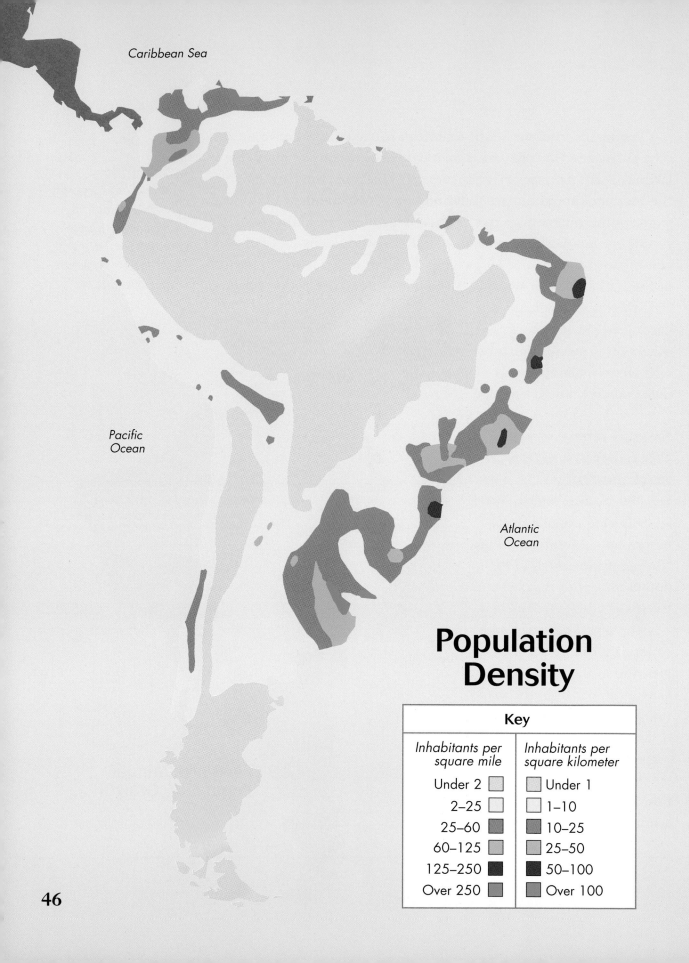

Caribbean Sea

Pacific
Ocean

Atlantic
Ocean

Population
Density

Key	
Inhabitants per square mile	Inhabitants per square kilometer
Under 2	Under 1
2–25	1–10
25–60	10–25
60–125	25–50
125–250	50–100
Over 250	Over 100

can see from the map on the opposite page. Nearly a third of all the people in South America live in Brazil. The greatest population density is found in pockets along Brazil's coast. There are also pockets of dense population in eastern Argentina, central Chile, and along the northern coasts of Colombia and Venezuela.

Per Capita GDP

Gross Domestic Product (GDP) is the total output of a country—all products and labor. Dividing the monetary value of a country's GDP by its population gives the per capita (per person) GDP. This figure represents the average annual income of that country's people. Generally speaking, more industrialized countries have a higher GDP—and a better economy—than less industrialized countries.

For example, Argentina, one of the most industrialized countries in South America, had an estimated 1994 per capita GDP of $7,990. Bolivia, with its minimal industrial base, is the poorest nation in South America. Bolivia's estimated per capita GDP was $2,370.

A Closer Look

You might expect a country's capital city to have a large population, but this is not always the case. If a capital is dominated by government buildings, the population may be small. If a capital is also a manufacturing or agricultural center, or a port, then it is more likely to have a large population. Compare the population density map on the opposite page with the major cities map on page 34. Which cities are in the most densely populated areas? How many of them are capital cities? Is there something other than government that makes these cities important? Look at the transportation routes map on page 48 for one explanation.

◀◀ *Opposite: Most of South America's pockets of dense population are along the coast of Brazil.*

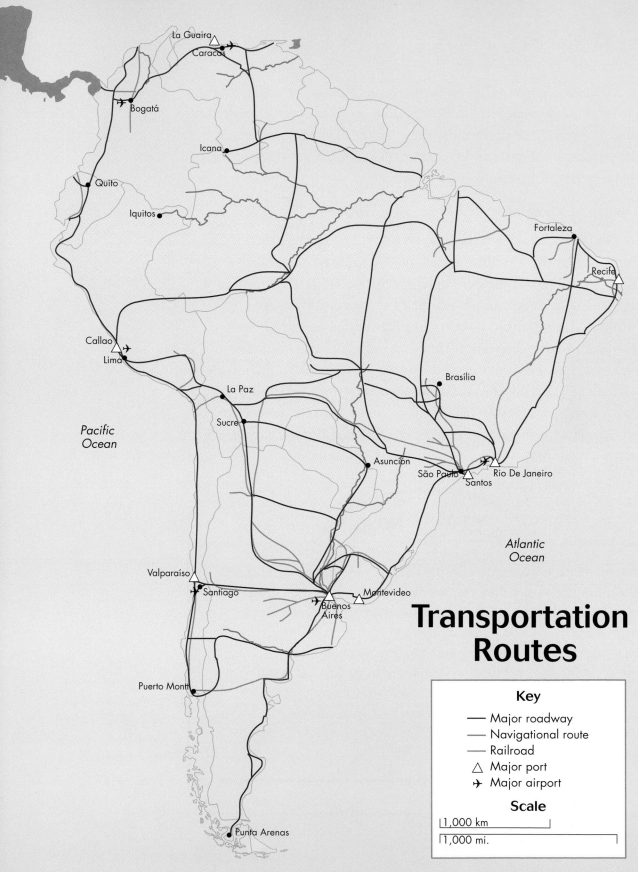

Caribbean Sea

La Guaira △
Caracas ●✈

Bogatá ●✈

Icana ●

Quito ●

Iquitos ●

Fortaleza ●

Recife ●△

Callao ●
Lima ●✈

La Paz ●

Sucre ●

Brasília ●

Pacific
Ocean

Asunción ●

São Paulo ●△ Rio De Janeiro ●
Santos △

Atlantic
Ocean

Valparaíso △
Santiago ●✈

Montevideo ●
Buenos
Aires ✈

Puerto Montt ●

Transportation
Routes

Punta Arenas ●

Key

— Major roadway
— Navigational route
— Railroad
△ Major port
✈ Major airport

Scale

| 1,000 km |
| 1,000 mi. |

3

Mapping the World Through Which We Move

In addition to showing us the physical and political characteristics of the world, maps can also have a more practical "hands on" purpose: They can assist us in moving through our world. Whether the world is an entire continent, a single city, or the second floor of an art museum, different maps provide us with the information we need to get from one point to another.

Maps Show the Way

Whenever we want to get from one place to another, maps can help us plan our routes by showing the options that are available. Maps show where roads are located and what kind of roads they are. They can also tell us whether we can take an airplane, train, bus, or other form of transportation to get there. Once we reach our destination, maps again can help us plan how best to get around—on foot, by car, or by some kind of public transportation.

Creating Road and City Maps

To create road maps and city maps, mapmakers (cartographers) look first for base data maps that accurately position points to be included

◀◀ *Opposite: Brazil has the most extensive highway system in South America.*

49

on the new map. These base maps might be acquired from the federal government, states, or cities. Aerial photographs may be taken to show if, and how, any areas may have changed since the base map was made.

Then, cartographers contact agencies that can provide specific information about street names—the names that will be the most help to a person traveling in the area. Other agencies are contacted to determine which buildings or other points of interest are important and should be included on the map of the area. Field work—actually visiting the area being mapped—adds useful first-hand information.

The Importance of Scale

Choosing the right scale for a map is an important step in making sure that the map will be as useful as possible.

To help people find their way around downtown Boston, for example, a cartographer would design a large-scale map that gives a close-up view of all the streets. But suppose someone wanted to drive from Philadelphia in eastern Pennsylvania to Pittsburgh in western Pennsylvania. Then a small-scale road map of the entire state would be more helpful than large-scale maps of all the cities between Philadelphia and Pittsburgh.

Scale also plays an important part in determining what is shown on a map. The smaller the scale, the more carefully cartographers must pick and choose the details that are being included. Careful selection is needed in order to keep a map from becoming too cluttered.

The transportation and city maps in this chapter provide still more ways to look at and learn about the South American continent, countries, and cities.

Transportation in South America

Despite the rugged terrain of much of South America, countries there are reasonably well connected by ground transportation—particularly roadways. You can see this by looking at the transportation map on page 48.

Roads

One of the most important roads in South America is the Pan American Highway. This highway, which has its beginnings at the United States–Mexico border, strings all the South American countries together by providing a link to their national road systems. The Pan American Highway, or an extension of it, also directly connects most South American capitals. Many of the roads marked in purple on the transportation map are part of the Pan American Highway.

Brazil has South America's most developed highway system. Many roads cluster in the southeast, where large urban areas, such as Rio de Janeiro, are located. Roads have also been built to provide access into and through the vast rain forest region, and to link the capital cities of various Brazilian states.

With the exception of the Pan American Highway system, and individual national road systems, most roads in South America are unpaved. The majority of South Americans don't own cars, and those who do usually live in urban areas. Buses provide passenger service both in and out of the cities, and trucks are used to transport freight.

Railroads

Argentina and Brazil have the largest rail systems in South America. On the whole, however, railroads are not a major part of the continent's transportation system. If you study the transportation map, you will see that South America's railroads, indicated in dark gray, generally do not run between cities. Instead, they link the coast to the interior. This pattern was established during colonial days, when railroads were built to take products from mines and plantations, in the interior, to coastal ports, from which these products were exported. Trains are still used primarily to transport freight rather than passengers.

Waterways

Oceans and rivers have played a major part in South America's transportation system from the earliest times. As the capitals and major cities map on page 34 shows, most of South America's major cities are located on or near the coast. Europeans settled there because of the difficulty of penetrating inland and because the climate was more comfortable along the coast. They relied on oceangoing ships for transporting freight from one point on the continent to another and to other parts of the world. During South America's colonial period, ships were also the primary means of transportation for European settlers who wanted to travel long distances. Rivers, indicated as navigational routes on the map, were used to move goods and people into and out of the interior.

Today, roads and airlines have lessened the importance of ships or boats for transporting people, except in remote areas. In terms of freight, however, river systems such as the Rio de la Plata in the southeast and the Amazon and Orinoco in the north are still valuable transportation routes. And oceangoing ships are still the primary method of exporting goods.

Airlines

Given the size of South America and its rugged terrain, airplanes offer the easiest and quickest way to travel long distances. Most countries offer international air service, and all major cities can be reached by plane. Brazil has South America's most extensive airline system, some of which is detailed on the map on page 60. In Brazil, which has about 1,500 airports, even small towns can be reached by air.

Other Transportation

In large, overcrowded cities all over the world, motor scooters—and feet!—are popular means of transportation. South America's urban centers are not exceptions. Some of the continent's larger cities, such as Buenos Aires, Argentina; Caracas, Venezuela; and Rio de Janeiro, Brazil operate subways. Outside the cities, people often walk from place to place, and they depend on animals such as donkeys or llamas to transport their goods.

The Cities of South America

Nearly all the capitals and major cities of South America were at one time administrative centers for European colonies, and as we noted earlier, these cities are along the coast.

In the Andean region, European settlers often built their cities on the sites of early native cities. For example, Cuzco, Peru, was the capital of the ancient Inca civilization. When Spaniards conquered the area, they erected many of their buildings on the stone foundations and walls of Inca palaces.

Cities with a Spanish heritage—such as the three to be discussed in this chapter—are usually built around a central square that is bordered by a church and government buildings. Streets are laid out in an orderly grid pattern. Cities with a Portuguese heritage, such as those in Brazil, follow a less rigid design.

▼ **Below:** *Buenos Aires is laid out in a grid pattern that is typical of Spanish cities.*

Buenos Aires

The layout of a Spanish city is easy to see on the map of Buenos Aires, the capital of Argentina. Among the city's many plazas is the Plaza de Mayo ("May Plaza"), in the southern section of the map. This plaza, the city's main square, commemorates the date—May 25, 1810—that Argentina first declared independence from Spain. (Formal independence came in 1816.) As is typical, church and government buildings surround the square.

The Catedral Metropolitana ("Metropolitan Cathedral"), on the north side, contains the tomb of General José de San Martín, who fought for Argentina's independence from Spain. To the west is El Cabildo, the government building where independence was declared. The Casa Rosada ("Pink House") is the present-day office of the president. In colonial days, it served as a fort to protect Buenos Aires from an invasion.

Notice the broad avenue running north and south through the center of the city. The name of this street—Avenida 9 de Julio ("July 9 Avenue")—honors the date in 1816 when Argentina formally became independent of Spain. The beautiful avenue, with grassy center sections and huge fountains spaced along it, helped Buenos Aires earn the nickname "The Paris of South America." The obelisk in the center of the Plaza de la Republica is set on the spot where the first flag of independence was flown.

▶ *Right: A 70-foot (21-meter) obelisk is at the center of the Plaza de la Republica in Buenos Aires.*

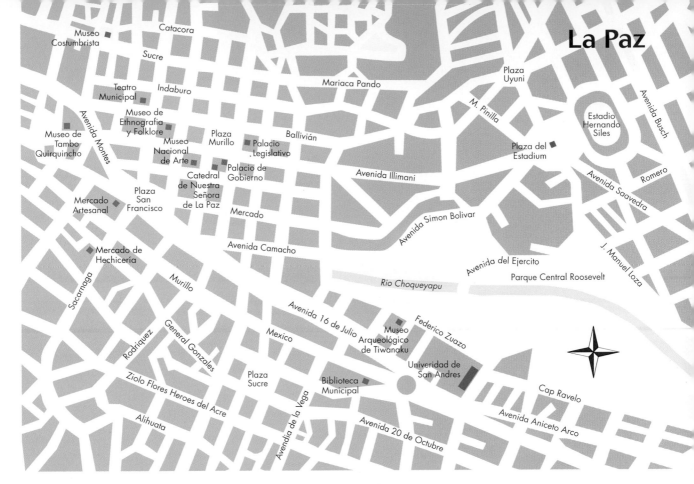

Map labels:
Museo Costumbrista · Catacora · Sucre · Mariaca Pando · Plaza Uyuni · La Paz · M. Pinilla · Avenida Busch · Teatro Municipal · Indaburo · Estadio Hernando Siles · Museo de Ethnografia y Folklore · Avenida Montes · Plaza Murillo · Ballivián · Plaza del Estadium · Avenida Saavedra · Museo de Tambo Quirquincho · Museo Nacional de Arte · Palacio Legislativo · Romero · Catedral de Nuestra Señora de La Paz · Palacio de Gobierno · Avenida Illimani · Mercado Artesanal · Plaza San Francisco · Mercado · Avenida Simon Bolivar · J. Manuel Loza · Mercado de Hechicería · Avenida Camacho · Avenida del Ejercito · Parque Central Roosevelt · Sacarnaga · Murillo · Rio Choqueyapu · Rodriquez · General Gonzales · Mexico · Avenida 16 de Julio · Federico Zuazo · Museo Arqueológico de Tiwanaku · Ziolo Flores Heroes del Acre · Plaza Sucre · Biblioteca Municipal · Univeridad de San Andres · Cap Ravelo · Alihuata · Avendia de la Vega · Avenida 20 de Octubre · Avenida Aniceto Arco

▲ **Above:** *Many of La Paz's museums are in the north-western section of the map.*

The Teatro Colón, three blocks north of the plaza on the west side of the avenue, houses an opera house and concert hall. The huge Plaza San Martín in the northeast part of the city contains a statue of Argentina's freedom fighter General José de San Martín, and is a popular gathering spot for tourists and residents alike.

La Paz

La Paz, the administrative capital of Bolivia, sits in a bowl-shaped valley on a plateau high in the Andes. At an altitude of about 12,000 feet (3,658 meters) above sea level, La Paz is the world's highest capital. Within the city are the remains of an ancient civilization, the Tiahuanaco. The Tiahuanaco culture, centered on the shores of near-by Lake Titicaca, was at its height from about A.D. 400 to 900. Stone carvings from the Tiahuanaco ruins are displayed in the Plaza del Estadium outside Estadio Hernanado Siles, La Paz's soccer stadium, in the upper right corner of the map above. The Museo Arqueológico de

▲ *Above:* La Paz is the highest capital city in the world.

Tiwanaku ("Tiahuanaco Museum"), in the south-eastern section of the map contains other artifacts from this civilization.

The street just south of Federico Zuazo, Avenida 16 de Julio, was named for July 16, 1809. This is the date of one of the first uprisings against Spain by the citizens of La Paz. As you have seen in the map of Buenos Aires, naming streets for historic dates, as well as people, is common in Latin American countries. The area of the city just north of Avenida 16 de Julio, in the northwest section of the map, is where you'll find many of La Paz's museums. Among them are the Museo de Etnografia y Folklore ("Folklore and Ethnography Museum"), which contains exhibits on Bolivia's native cultures; the Museo Nacional de Arte ("National Art Museum"), which houses paintings and sculptures; and the Museo Costumbrista ("Museum of Customs"), which depicts the lifestyle and customs of early La Paz through a series of miniature sculptures. The Teatro Municipal, also located in this area, hosts ballet and symphonic programs.

Central to this section of La Paz is the Plaza Murillo, built on the spot where the revolutionary hero Pedro Domingo Murillo was hanged. Grouped around the plaza in typical Spanish style are the Palicio de Gobierno ("Presidential Palace"), the Palacio Legislativo ("Legislative Palace"), and the Catedral de Nuestra Señora de La Paz ("Cathedral of Our Lady of La Paz").

To the south, in the vicinity of the Plaza San Francisco, are two special markets. The Mercado Artesanal ("Craft Market") features native handicrafts such as woven blankets and ceremonial masks. Herbs, charms, and other items important to native magic and healing rituals are sold in the Mercado de Hechichería ("Witchcraft Market").

Caracas

If you look at the map of Caracas, the capital of Venezuela, you will
see the orderly grid pattern and wide avenues of a Spanish city. The
grandest street, the Avenida Bolívar, is named after the "Great
Liberator" Simon Bolívar, who was born in Caracas. Many important
landmarks in the city have some connection with Bolívar. To the west,
the Plaza Bolívar was built in 1567, but it was renamed in Bolívar's
honor more than 200 years later. His tomb is located in El Panteon
Nacional, which is almost directly north, near the top of the map.

To the west of Bolívar's birthplace (Casa Natal de Libertador) is
El Capitolio, the home of the National Congress. Covered with a
gold dome, it is a city landmark. Paintings of Venezuelan patriots

▼ **Below:** *The Jardín
Botánico ("Botanical
Garden") contributes a lot
of open space to Caracas.*

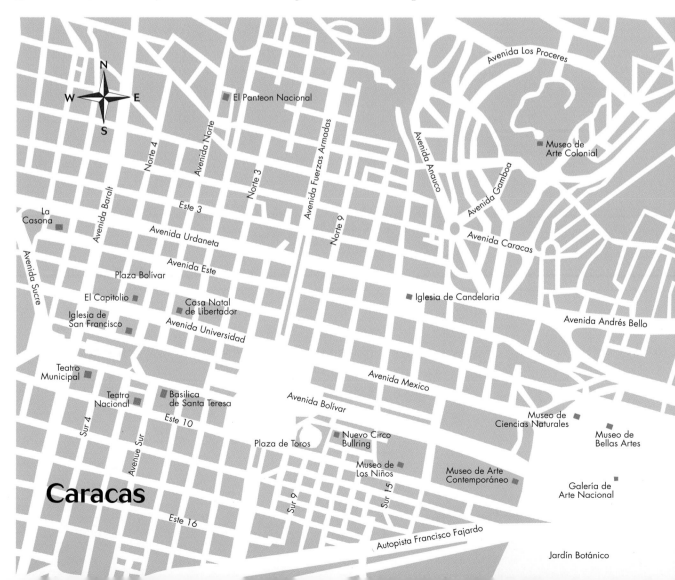

Caracas

Jardín Botánico

▲ *Above:* The wide
Avenida Bolívar cuts through
the center of Caracas.

and scenes from an important battle for independence are found inside the building. La Casona, to the northwest, is the president's mansion. South of the El Capitolio is Iglesia de San Francisco ("St. Francis Church"), where Bolívar received the title of "Great Liberator" in 1813.

To the southeast is the Basilica de Santa Teresa, one of the most important churches in Caracas. Venezuela's oldest statue of Christ is found here. Another important church is Candelaria, which is located in the center of the map. José Gregorio Hernandez, who was declared a saint for his treatment and care of the poor, is entombed in Candelaria.

Among the many museums in Caracas are those shown on the map near the Jardín Botánico ("Botanical Garden") in the southeast part of the city. The Museo de Bellas Artes ("Museum of Fine Arts") features the work of Venezuelan artists. Heading counterclockwise, you'll notice the Museo de Ciencias Naturales ("the Natural Science Museum"), Museo de Los Niños ("Children's Museum") and Museo de Arte Contemporáneo ("Museum of Contemporary Art"), which specializes in twentieth-century works.

Other Maps and Guides

In addition to road and city street maps, there are many other maps and guides that are useful to us in moving through our world. There are navigational charts for boaters, maps that show special points of interest, such as all the caves in a state or all the parks or monuments in a city. Floor plans that guide you through famous buildings and museums are another kind of map. And, there are trail guides for hikers, bikers, skiers, and horseback riders.

However you choose to get around our vast and complicated world—and wherever you choose to go—you will always find that maps will help you do it much more easily.

It's About Time

When we travel, we move through time as well as space. The maps you have been consulting so far in this chapter, and many of the others in this book, can help you get from place to place—or move through space. The map of South America's time zones on this page helps you see whether you will also move through time when you travel.

The world is divided into 24 time zones that begin at the prime meridian, the line of longitude passing through Greenwich, England. This point is called Greenwich Mean Time. There are 12 zones west of Greenwich and 12 zones east of it. To figure out the time in

Key

- 2 hours behind Greenwich Mean Time
- 3 hours behind Greenwich Mean Time
- 3.5 hours behind Greenwich Mean Time
- 4 hours behind Greenwich Mean Time
- 5 hours behind Greenwich Mean Time

Caribbean Sea

Caracas
VENEZUELA
Georgetown
GUYANA
SURINAME
Paramaribo
FRENCH GUIANA
Bogotá
COLOMBIA
Quito
ECUADOR
Manaus
Belém
PERU
BRAZIL
Lima
BOLIVIA
La Paz
Salvador
Brasília
CHILE
PARAGUAY
Asunción
Rio de Janeiro
ARGENTINA
Atlantic Ocean
Santiago
URUGUAY
Buenos Aires
Montevideo
Pacific Ocean

South American Time Zones

◄ *Left: Uruguay is in its own time zone, just two hours behind Greenwich Mean Time.*

Caribbean Sea

To Miami

Caracas

VENEZUELA

GUYANA

To Mexico

Bogotá

SURINAME

FRENCH
GUIANA

Bôa Vista

To Panama &
Los Angeles

Macapá

COLOMBIA

Belém

São Luis

ECUADOR

Manaus

Santarém

Fortaleza

Iquitos

Tefé

Marabá

Imperatriz

Teresina

Natal

To Lisbon, Portugal

Tabatinga

Araguaína

Juazeiro
do Norte

João Pessoa

Cruzeiro do Sul

Campina
Grande

Recife

To Milan, Italy

Porto Velho

BRAZIL

Petrolina

Maceió

To Paris, France

PERU

Rio Branco

Aracaju

To Lagos, Portugal

Salvador

La Paz

BOLIVIA

Cuiabá

Goiânia

Brasília

Montes
Claros

Ilhéus

Corumbá

Uberlândia

Uberaba

Vitória

Pacific
Ocean

Campo
Grande

Belo Horizonte

PARAGUAY

São
Paulo

Rio de Janeiro

Atlantic
Ocean

CHILE

Foz do
Iguaçu

Curitiba

Asunción

Joinville

Navegantes

Florianópolis

Criciúma

Porto Alegre

ARGENTINA

URUGUAY

Buenos Aires

Brazil's
Air Routes

another part of the world, subtract an hour from the time in your own zone for each zone to the west of you, and add an hour for each zone to the east.

As you can see from the map on page 59, South America has five different zones. The westernmost zone, colored pink, is five hours behind Greenwich Mean Time. If it is noon in Greenwich, it is 7 o'clock in the morning in Colombia. The East Coast of the United States is in the same time zone as Colombia.

Taking to the Air

When you plan a trip, you consult different, specialized maps depending on how you will be traveling. If you are going to fly, you will need a map such as the one of Brazil's air routes on the opposite page. This map tells you which South American cities can be reached by air, and which Brazilian cities are hubs. A hub offers flights to a wide variety of locations. The pattern of air routes out of such cities looks like spokes radiating from the hub of a wheel.

As mentioned earlier, Brazil has South America's most extensive airline system. It is easy to see from the map of Brazil's air routes that Manaus, Brasilia, São Paulo, and Salvador are hub cities with many air connections to other cities. If you were to fly to Brazil, chances are pretty good that you would be flying into one of those cities first.

A Closer Look

Transportation maps tell us how to get around in a particular place. In this chapter you also have a map that tells you when you would arrive in various places.

Look again at the time zones and air routes maps. A flight from Cruzeiro do Sul, in western Brazil, to Belém, on the coast, takes five hours. What time will you arrive in Belém if you leave Cruzeiro do Sul at noon?

◀◀ *Opposite:* Brazil has four hub cities: Manaus, Brasília, São Paulo, and Salvador.

Glossary

acid rain Rain that has collected waste gases from the atmosphere and is damaging to the environment.

colonization Occupying another country to make use of its resources.

deforestation Large-scale clearing of forested land, which may die as a result.

desertification The creation of desert conditions as a result of long droughts, overgrazing, or soil erosion.

drought A long period without rainfall.

export Something sold and shipped to another country.

Gross Domestic Product (GDP) The total output of a country; all products and labor.

hardwood Broadleaf trees (see **softwood**).

indigenous Original to a particular place.

isthmus A narrow strip of land connecting two large land masses.

pampa A treeless, fertile grassy plain.

per capita per person (literally, "per head").

plateau A large, mostly level, area of land that is higher than the land surrounding it.

salinization The process by which nutrients are washed from the soil by over irrigation, leaving the soil encrusted with salts.

shifting agriculture Farming a small area of land until the soil is nearly worn out, then moving on, leaving the first area to grow wild and renew itself naturally.

softwood Coniferous, or cone-bearing, trees.

subsistence farming Growing crops or raising animals for personal use, rather than for sale or trade.

Further Reading

Blue, Rose and Corinne Naden. *Andes Mountains*. Wonders of the World (series). Austin, TX: Raintree Steck-Vaughn, 1995.

Central and South America. Vol. 6 of Lands and Peoples (series). Danbury, CT: Grolier, Inc., 1997.

Gofen, Ethel Caro. *Argentina*. Cultures of the World (series). New York: Marshall Cavendish, 1991.

Machado, Ana Maria. *Exploration into Latin America*. Parsippany, NJ: Silver Burdett Press, 1995.

Morrison, Marion. *Brazil—Country Fact Files*. Austin, TX: Raintree Steck-Vaughn, 1994.

Pateman, Robert. *Bolivia*. Cultures of the World (series). New York: Marshall Cavendish, 1991.

Pickering, Marianne. *Chile*. Exploring Cultures of the World (series). Tarrytown, NY: Marshall Cavendish, 1997.

South America. Vol. 5 of the Encyclopedia of World Geography. New York: Marshall Cavendish, 1994.

Index

Page numbers for illustrations are in boldface.